L.I.F.E.

Living In a Fragmented Existence

Charita N. Whitaker

Cover design by Anthony Garcia

This book is dedicated in loving memory

To my grandfather

Harold Frasier Sr.

(11/28/40-11/25/01)

You made sure that you taught your children and grandchildren aspects of life. You were hard on us at times, but we know that was because you loved us and you wanted us to get to our place of destiny. You were big on us having goals and aspirations. Thank you for taking the time to teach us the many lessons of life. We all will continue to live on in your legacy. I will always love you.

&

To my mother

Carmen Yolanda Whitaker

(11/05/66-04/06/07)

To my dear loving mother who taught me all she knew about life. I thank you for your teachings, and the values and morals you instilled in me. You planted a seed and nurtured it so that I could be the woman God destined me to be. The many talks we had will never be forgotten. You took the time to cultivate my talent and to encourage me in all that I wanted to do. You will eternally live on in my heart and soul, and always be my angel that was taken too soon. Thanks for being the best mom you could be. I am who I am today because of your love! I will continue to strive to do my best to make you proud. I will always love and miss you. May your soul forever rest in peace.

Why I'm Not A Dancer

(Dedicated To My Mother)

Strong, graceful free strides.

Angelic movements.

Their bodies speak a language,

It tells a story.

A story that only a dancer

can understand.

Such elegance and grace.

Their body interprets

what their mind is thinking.

A clear and precise way

of speaking to other dancers.

I understand their art,

but my body is unable to do their work.

They are masters of their trade.

But me, I am connected to writers.

Their words jump up

at me like my own thinking.

Their language becomes my language,

our thoughts connect.

My hand interprets what my mind thinks

it writes them down in words.

You see, writing is my language,

my interpretation of me.

It is the trade that I master,

and that is the reason

Why I am not a dancer.

A Note To The Reader

Dear Reader,

Let me start by saying thank you for investing in this book. I wrote this collection of poetry for you. For adolescents all over the world feeling like they are struggling on their own and no one understands the difficulties they face. This book is an outlet for your voice to be heard. To let the world know, "hey, we have problems too".

I wrote the first poem for this book when I was fourteen years old. At the time I didn't know why I was writing except that I wanted to express my emotions. Some of the issues in this book I have dealt with first hand; death, self-esteem, and self-worth. While others, I was able to take a glimpse through others experiences but feel it as if it were my own. This book is not meant for my views to be forced upon you, but rather for you to perhaps look at life's challenges in another perspective. I hope that after you finish reading this collection you can come up with an overall positive message that will benefit you in your everyday struggle. Always remember, what you choose to live with is up to you! Welcome to the book of L.I.F.E.

Table of Contents

Table of Contents

Table of Contents

Table of Contents

Life

What is life?

Why am I here?

What am I to do?

Do I belong here?

Am I doing my very best?

Am I doing everything in

my power to reach success?

This is my life and I must

take control.

And strive to achieve my

greatest goal.

I need to take all that life

can give,

because that's the only way

I'll learn to live.

But what is it all about?

Do I know without a doubt?

Do I know what I can do,

to help people like me and you?

Do I know all the trials

I must face,

In order to be a good person

in this human race?

Life is something that we must

live.

Which we shouldn't take but

only give.

But we must do what

we know is right.

And strive to live with

all our might.

Sometimes it will be easy,

but hard it shall also be.

But we must make it through

in order to succeed.

So when life seems hard

And it seems rough.

You must be strong and

you must be tough.

We can only live one time.

You must live

your life.

And I must

live mine.

Individuality

You do not like me,

Oh well that is truly good for you.

You hate the way I look and act

because I do not do what you do.

Well, I do not need you to like me.

I am proud of who I am.

I do not care what others think.

I do not live my life for them.

So don't think I'm going to change,

to conform to your likes and ways.

I am going to continue to be who I am

until the end of my days.

So continue to say what you want to say.

And think what you want of me.

But I'm going to do what I want to do.

And be who I want to be.

Free

There is a struggle

to overcome.

A need to be fulfilled.

To soar high above

the doubts and unbelief.

The adjustment of pain

is the beginning of love.

To see what's not

And truly believe there is

Trying to thrive....

To be.....

A dream to live

What I Want

I do not want to be

a part of a race.

I do not want to be

a statistic.

I do not want to be

a ratio.

I do not want to be

a stereotype.

I do not want to be

a problem.

I want to be

the solution.

I want to be

a help to better the world.

But most of all,

I want to be

an individual-

I want to be me.

Different

Sometimes it seems that

I'm all alone in this maze

they call the world.

There seems to be no one else

like me.

I am different.

I stick out like a sore thumb.

And for this I am punished.

Instead of being congratulated

for being unique,

I am scorned for being one of a kind.

My peers don't like my originality.

They hate who I am.

They can't stand the fact

that I won't conform to their ways.

So they

tease me,

taunt me,

mock me,

and beat me,

I am abused.

Their beatings hurt,

but their words hurt more.

Their words burrow into my

heart and into my soul.

It cuts me and leaves deep wounds.

The pain is too much to bear.

It's more than I can handle.

They treat me like I'm not human,

as if I don't hurt.

They do not understand the

damage they cause.

If only they could feel my pain,

if only they knew

what it's like to be me.

The Maze

The Right....

The Wrong....

The In....

The Out....

A yearning

To learn,

is it love

That's missing in life?

The option

to agree,

the understanding of it all.

To be able

to choose....

To search,

to find out.

The purpose

to belong

which is the reason to give

Solutions to find…..

A life to be lived.

What's The Difference?

I am not liked because

of the color of my skin.

But no one wants to judge me

for the person that is within.

They do not see that

my eyes are like theirs.

They do not see that we

cry the same tears.

They do not see that

we both have one nose.

They do not see through

our veins red blood flows.

They do not see that we

both have two hands.

It's the simple things

they just can't seem to

understand-we're not so different.

Image

Imagine…

A world without hate.

A world without violence.

A world without skin color,

but just the human race.

Imagine…

A world with love.

A world with peace.

A world with hope,

and smiles across everyone's faces.

Oh what a beautiful world

this would be,

and what a wonderful image

It would be to see,

If we could all live as one in

harmony.

Communication

Unable to hear the sounds of

the world,

but able to see the beauty.

Unable to hear people's words

but able to see them.

I have so much to say,

but no one willing to listen.

So many questions to ask and

no one to answer.

My hands are ready to talk,

my eyes are willing to listen,

but only if there were someone else

to communicate with me.

Qualities

Trustworthy, loyal, and honest.

Able to pick you up when

you're down.

Able to understand you.

Concerned about your well-being.

Willing to help you in any way

they can.

Not jealous of you,

but happy for what you have

and what you accomplish.

Able to correct you when you're wrong,

Able to compliment you on

good works.

They truly understand the value

of friendship,

and what it means to be

a friend.

Verbal Weapon

Hate.

A word that cuts like

a sword.

It can kill.

It can destroy.

It can manipulate,

can cause friends to

become enemies.

It eats away at our

hearts and souls

causing damage to our being.

Hatred

shatters lives,

destroys hope and innocence.

Hate is a word that causes somuch damage.

It is a weapon,

a weapon all on its own.

<u>Letters</u>

1/03

Dear Boyfriend,

I've found the right one for me.

And eternally I will be with thee

to cherish the love we have grown to share.

And knowing that you'll always be here

I am ready to move on,

take another step.

For you I am willing to lose self-respect.

I am ready to be intimate with you,

I'm sure that it's the right thing to do.

I know that you love me and

by this it will show.

It will cause our relationship to

flourish and grow.

You have been ready for this

for such a long time.

And now I am willing,

I believe it will be fine.

So I am ready for it to happen,

the time is right.

It's gonna be one special spectacular night.

Dear Girlfriend,

I can't believe you're ready,

I can't believe it's true.

I can't believe I'm gonna show

how much I love you.

So now you are ready,

you finally trust me.

I can't wait,

I'm excited as can be.

I'm so glad you're willing,

and yes the time is right.

It's gonna be a wonderful

spectacular night.

Dear Diary,

5:06 pm

It has been 3 months since

my intimate night.

But something is wrong,

something's not right.

I think I am pregnant but

how could this be?

I am so young

this can't happen to me.

I'm going to take a home

pregnancy test,

and I hope everything turns

out for the best.

I can't believe this happened,

it cannot be true.

But the stick shows two pink lines

and not one blue.

I am pregnant, why did things

turn out this way?

I wish I could go back

and change the events of that day.

Dear Boyfriend,

I am so scared,

I don't know what to do.

I think that it's time that

I finally tell you.

I am 4 months pregnant,

I thought you should know,

because pretty soon I'm gonna

start to show.

I can't seem to think,

things are moving too fast.

I wish we could go back

and change the past.

Dear Girl,

I am so shocked,

I can't believe it's true.

but I can't help, I don't know

what to do.

I'm sorry that things turned

out this way,

but we can't blame it on

that one day.

We were only intimate one time

and we used protection,

so this child can't be mine.

I truly feel bad for the predicament

that you're in,

but please don't call or

write me again.

Dear Diary,

My heart is hurting,

I'm in so much pain.

He told me never to write him

again.

I can't believe he's going

to leave me all alone.

He needs to help,

I didn't make this child on my own.

He said he loved me,

but that's not true.

He only loved me for

what he could do.

I'm so sorry I believed

his line.

I wish I could go

back into time.

Dear Diary,

I finally told my family,

they didn't believe me at first.

But when I told them again,

they were really hurt.

My mom couldn't stop crying,

she cried all night.

She said she wish I

would've thought things out right.

She said now my life is all off track

And wished I could go

and change things back.

RE: Girls Learn From Me

To Whom It May Concern:

I was in love and I thought

he was in love with me.

But things didn't turn out

the way I thought it would be.

I wanted to be intimate and

try something new.

And I did something which

I knew I shouldn't do.

I made a choice that was not wise.

And didn't think of the

consequences that would arise.

After he found out I was pregnant,

my ex left me all alone.

And now I have to raise our newborn

daughter on my own.

I'm so young,

I haven't graduated from school.

And things are much harder now,

I don't think I'll make it through.

Instead of taking one step

forward, I took a step back.

And I have to work hard

to get my life back on track.

I thought I had a guy

who would stay by my side,

but he only stayed long

enough for a ride.

And you're probably thinking

you have a guy who will stay.

But you can't be sure

until something happens one day.

So girls I think it's time

that you learn from me.

Do not be intimate without

sure guarantee.

And the surest guarantee is abstinence.

That's the only way

you'll be safe in every sense.

Unexpected

Life isn't always as it seems;

the ups and downs,

the crushed dreams.

Full of disappointment and agony...

What's the point?

The point of being here,

of living.

Wanting everything to be ok,

but then the struggle.

Trying to overcome the struggles

but the struggles seem to overcome me.

All is not well.

I'm drowning in a sea of misery.

What is it

that will become of me?

All Grown Up

Being able to make choices,

choices that will affect our lives.

Knowing which path to take,

which decision to make.

Knowing what to do

and what not to do.

Not relying on anyone else

to make our decisions.

Having the ability to know

what's best for our lives.

That little moment when

the power

is in our hands,

and we can become

directors

of our lives.

Choices

The desolate

place

is where I'm destined

to be.

Lost in a

world where

there is

no peace of mind.

I'm stuck in confusion,

or is the confusion stuck in me?

Finding a way in,

knowing there's no way out.

The desert is my home,

surviving is the

key to my existence.

Frustration is my companion,

anger is my child.

We live together as one

in harmony.

The drive to live

is my will to be…………..

Forever

is not eternity………….

The desolate place

is where I'm destined to be.

<u>That Feeling</u>

Searching...

Looking....

Yearning....

Longing to fill

that empty space,

the void in my heart.

Hopefully,

one day someone

will come along

and give me

what I need,

something to hold on to,

something to give

me peace and hope.

Hopefully someday

soon,

I'll feel what I want

the most.

Feel that someone

cares about my being.

What I want

the most

is to be

loved.

<u>Identity Crisis</u>

I don't judge myself

according to my

standards.

But I judge myself

according to what

others think of me.

Every day I change

my personality

to conform to the

people around me.

That's just who I

Am-

Whatever they want

me to be.

I like what they like,

I do what they

do,

and I think what they

think.

I don't know who I am,

I am not me.

I am their clone,

their carbon-copy.

The Promise

Today, the sun came down

and kissed the earth,

blessing it with eternal beauty.

Making friends out of enemies,

taking all the bad and making

it good

and giving hope to those who've lost

it all.

The moon gleamed a little longer

lighting the way for those

who have been lost in the dark.

And the rain came to give water

to those who were thirsty.

Then the rainbow came bringing

the promise

that tomorrow

would be a better day.

Looking Back

Years have

passed away,

since the horrid

terrible days

of Jim Crow.

Our ancestors

fought, bled

and died

for their rights.

For their right

to be heard,

their right

to have justice,

their right to be

treated humane.

Although they were

forbidden to live,

and

forbidden to exist,

they continued to fight.

They fought for

our equality,

our justice,

our humanity.

Because of their struggle,

we have seen their dreams

and visions.

We have reaped from

their labor.

But the vision that

passed on,

has slipped

from our eyes.

No more pride do we have

for the things they couldn't do

We do not cherish our rights,

and celebrate their victory.

We let their struggle kill

their dreams for our lives.

They were slaves of their

time

but now we are "free".....

But we continue to live

in bondage.

It's time that we take

our dreams and visions back.

It's time that we go back to

the old times

and remember how far we have come,

and how much further we have to go.

But in order to advance,

we have to indulge

in the opportunities that we have now

or our future will pass us by.

It's time to show our gratitude

for what our ancestors have done.

Don't let the blood that was shed

fall mercilessly in the grave,

don't let their dying be in vain.

Take a look back............................

__Family__

A strong non-destructive unit,

a solid foundation.

Unable to crumble.

but able to stand.

Loving, caring, and understanding.

Concerned and compassionate.

Interested in others feelings

and concerns.

Through the hard and tedious times

able to stand together.

They are many in numbers,

yet they stand as one.

They are strong, determined, and

undivided.

They are a family.

Tomorrow

Tomorrow

Is a new opportunity

for me to live another day,

to get rid of the old

memories of yesterday

Tomorrow

is a new experience,

A new adventure

to look forward to

Tomorrow is a wish,

tomorrow is a dream come true.

But who said tomorrow

would ever come?

So why should we leave

today's work undone.

No one can be sure

if tomorrow will ever show,

that is something

we just don't know.

Tomorrow......?????

Impoverished

Humanitarian

Despair,

suffering,

hardships.

Lack of essentials,

and longing for luxury.

Desperation and hope

for the future.

The ability to fulfill

personal desires.

Longing to be a part of this

material judgmental world,

so that one day,

I can be a help

to someone whose shoes

I was once in.

Love Is A Crazy Thing

Love is a crazy thing.

It makes you ecstatic and silly,

happy and sad.

It makes you fun and adventurous

ambitious and mad.

Sometimes you'll find that love

will make you cry.

And most of the time you won't

even know why.

These are all the things that love

will do.

Boy,

love is a crazy thing.

I Cry

I cry

when I'm happy.

I cry

when I'm sad.

I cry

when I'm lonely.

I cry

when I'm mad.

All my pain and hurt flows

when my tears drop.

That's my way of expressing

myself through the fallen drops.

Sometimes I sit and cry

and I can't explain why.

It's like a way of relieving

pain stress

and dealing with my

emotional mess.

That is why,

sometimes I cry.

What Kind of World?

What kind of world

do we live in,

where people commit crimes

no matter the cost?

What kind of world

do we live in,

where people will murder without

any remorse?

What kind of world

do we live in,

where children are

being snatched away?

What kind of world

do we live in,

where children are bringing

guns to school each day?

What kind of world

do we live in,

where people are

in need of food?

What kind of world

do we live in,

where we see more bad deeds

than deeds of good?

What kind of world

do we live in,

where people won't do right

but rather do wrong?

What kind of world

do we live in,

where we can't even

get along?

It's time that we take

a good look

at what we've done

to the world

and what we have become.

It's time that someone

takes a good look

and tell me

please tell me,

what kind of world do we live in?

<u>Being You</u>

In society

being different

is a crime.

Our personality,

and actions must mock

those around us.

There is no need for

assortment.

What we see is what we

become.

Is it that we are

afraid to be individuals?

Afraid to stand alone in a world

of clones?

What's the sense of living

if we can't live our own lives?

Individuality is precious.

And everyone is an individual.

But what is unique?

Can we be different

if we act the same?

Are we stuck in a world

with no imagination

or form?

When I look at you

do I see me?

Are we reflections

of each other?

How can we mingle

if there is no difference?

How can we converse

if you and I are one?

Without any

selection of style

there would be no

variance.

In this world,

in our era and time,

diversity is a necessity

and

individuality is creativity.

<u>Conscience</u>

It lurks in the shadows,

pondering my every move.

Contemplating my decisions

and choices.

It dissects all of my motives

trying to find hidden agendas.

It enters my thoughts

unexpectedly.

It takes over my mind,

my heart, and my soul.

It steers me in the path of

right and not wrong,

Everywhere I go it's right

beside me,

Giving me the help

and confidence

I need.

My Name Is......

I do not discriminate

I come for the old as

well as the young,

I come for every nationality

and ethnicity.

I come expectedly

and sometimes I come unexpectedly.

Sometimes I come by sickness,

such as AIDS, cancer and

heart disease.

Other times I come through,

car accidents, gun shots and overdoses.

I take the guilty as well

as the innocent

I have no conscience

only victims

My name is......

DEATH

66

One Nation

We watched in terror

as the towers began to fall.

And when the towers fell

so did our courage

We were afraid.

Afraid of the unseen,

afraid of the unknown.

No longer could we walk down

the street without a glance

at the sky.

Every time a plane was heard,

we had to make sure it was

still in the air.

Our faith was shaken,

our security was taken.

On that one day we lost so much,

our family, friends, courage

and assurance.

But there was one thing we did

not lose,

and that was our freedom.

Although we walked in fear,

we refused to give up our liberty.

A nation that was griped

by shock and horror became united.

We comforted each other in the time

of loss and despair.

The terrorist had a plan to change America forever,

and yes they succeeded.

We became a country fortified in unity.

In the time of crisis,

America proved to the world just

who we are

"One nation under God with Liberty"

*Dedicated to all those who lost their lives on 9/11**

Stand Up

Stand up

and be counted.

Let your voice

be heard.

A sound

with uplifting thoughts.

With darkness

all around,

be the light of hope.

Find joy and

peace in your well being.

Give thanks

for the things

that are all around.

Love all, even

those who cannot love.

Be the exception

to the negative.

Be the acceptor

of the positive.

Be the leader of

today.

Take one step to change

tomorrow.

Do all things

that can be done.

Be that voice in the night.

The Many Faces Of Life

Life is a teacher

an instructor.

Life is a game

that must be mastered.

Life is a journey

an adventure.

Life is a road map

to your future.

Life is a hidden rainbow

an unknown treasure.

Life is a joyous book

with certain anguish and pleasure.

Life is a fable

with many lessons.

Life is a gift

an abundant blessing.

Confident?

Possessor

of a mountain

but cannot climb.

Believer of the

wind,

but can't feel its air.

Holder of the

priceless,

But do not know

the worth.

The ability to fly,

but can't leave

the ground.

Able to see all

things,

but yet still

so blind.

Hope for all things,

but *still* no faith?

A Brain on Drugs

Abuse, batter, kill, destroy.

That's what is done to me.

One little puff or sniff

is taking away my ability to function.

I can't think right

therefore I can't act right.

I'm slowly slipping away.

I'm being destroyed

just for a couple of hours of 'happiness'.

They don't know what they're doing to me.

And how can they?

I'm too messed up to tell them.

I'm afraid that just one more time

and I'm going to be dead.

And when I die, they will die too.

Life as they know it will be over.

Can someone please help me?

I am a brain on drugs

One More Day

Going out to hang with his friends.

Didn't know his life was gonna

come to an end.

He was only nineteen

a lot of things he had barely seen.

Someone shot him in the head

and immediately he was dead.

Too bad his life came to an end,

only because he was going to see a friend.

A lot of things he will not be able to do

all because of someone cruel.

They took his precious life away

only if he could've lived to see

one more day.

****

When is the violence going to end?

When are we not goin' to let this happen?

When is the nation going to step-in and say

"*Enough is enough, no more violence*

Can we take

Being violent is a big mistake."

Many lives are taken away

because someone is shot and killed

each day.

It's time to see what can be done

to save the lives of everyone.

Committing an act of violence is not cool.

It is only done by fools.

So before you take out that gun or knife

and take away someone else's life,

think and see all the grief you will cause.

Think,.

Think,.

And just pause.

Today I Shed a Tear

Today I shed a tear

for someone very dear.

Who knew wrong from right

but wanted to mess up his life.

When I saw his face he was not

the person I once knew.

Something had changed and it was

not the fact that he had grew.

He had no value on his life,

it was as if it had no price.

He walked around without a care

and he lived his life as a dare.

He was even in a gang

which he thought was a good thing.

"They're my family", he used to say

They take care of me everyday."

But then one day he had a fight

and his gang was nowhere in sight.

He was alone with someone

who had a knife

and that person took away his life.

It is so sad and it is truly a shame

that he had to die

And there is no one to blame.

There's so many things he could've done

instead he wanted to have fun.

Now everyone is in so much pain

Because they will never see him again

Today,

I shed a tear.

A Secret Not Shared

Carried around

their mouths

like a caged bird,

burdening their

hearts like

a thousand tons.

Knowing the

dark truth-

The truth was never shared.

It hardened their hearts,

troubling those who cared.

The gruesome truth

stared them

in the face,

yet the truth

remained hidden.

Not one mouth

opened to

say a word-

To let the words fly out

and exist.

They thought

they were protectors,

helping out.
Instead they were

aiding in killing a soul.

For the one

they were

keeping lost their life,

because of the

truth no one brought

to light.

Many mourned

and cried

for the one who died,

everyone felt anguish

and guilt inside.

For they all began to

blame themselves.

They finally began to see

that maybe

if someone would've

said a word

things would've turned

out differently.

And they all sat

silent and still

because the end

results were exactly what

they feared.

And they all wished

a secret

they would've shared.

Peace

There's not one day

that goes by,

That someone doesn't cry

because,

their father was murdered,

their mother was robbed,

their sister was battered,

their brother was stabbed,

their daughter was raped,

their son was kidnapped.

This list can go on and on.

But when are we going to

make this list shorter,

so that these crimes

exist no longer.

Will we finally be at ease,

if we have a world with total

peace?

Premature Death

I'm in a world of

total darkness.

I see no light.

I want to emerge

and find the day,

but I'm forever in

the night.

I want to enjoy

life again.

I want to experience

new things.

I want to be happy.

I want to exist.

Carefree days

are what I want again.

If only I could

start anew.

If only I could live again

My Color Is Not Me

You judge me by the

color of my skin,

but you don't know

who I am.

You do not know the

life that I live.

You do not know

the amount of love I give.

You do not know

my personality.

You do not know my

pursuit of individuality.

You do not know

any of my philosophies.

You don't even know

me.

All you see is the color

of my skin.

But my color doesn't make up

who I am.

My color is not me.

It's only one of the shades

of the earth.

We Are......

We act as if

we are unable

to have the ability,

to act intelligently,

to behave respectably,

to let the world see,

that we are capable human beings.

We act as if

we are unable

to let our mind grow,

to let our knowledge show,

to let the world know,

that we are remarkable human beings.

We act as if

we are unable

to live above the stereotype,

to live a life we know is right,

to go one day without a fight,

to let the world know in fact,

that we are exceptional human beings.

We act as if

we are unable

to live a life of integrity,

to make choices responsibly,

to strive to be the best we can be,

to let the world see,

that we are

Capable..

Exceptional...

Remarkable....

Unstoppable human beings.

Destiny

Stuck

in a place

that needs to change.

The fear of the new

keeps me glued to the past.

The present holds

the unexpected

that has come to be expected.

Willing to give up on dreams

just to believe again.

The preparation of the future

has become my downfall.

What is it that I need?

Hoping and wishing for the

longing to be fulfilled.

To reach the place of rhapsody.....

But where does that lie?

Is it in the past or the future?

Or in the present with me?

A Story To Tell

It was around eleven o' clock

I was just arriving home

and what I saw made my heart stop.

Police cars and ambulances were all over the place

and I saw men with stretchers going into my gate.

I immediately ran to find out what was going on.

When I got inside I knew something was wrong.

My mom and dad were both in tears,

and the officers were whispering in

each other's ears.

I looked around past everyone's stares

and I saw men with stretchers

going up the stairs.

I ran past them to see what I could find,

when I saw my sister's room

I thought I'd lose my mind.

When I walked in her room

I couldn't believe what I saw.

My sister was lying dead sprawled

out on the floor.

I couldn't believe it,

I knew it couldn't be true.

But my sister's eyes were glazed

and her lips were pale blue.

My heart began to crumble,

I slumped down to the floor.

And the emergency medical technicians

were standing at the door.

They both held their heads down,

they were afraid to look my way.

And I was terrified and afraid of

what they were going to say.

One of them stepped forward

and gently touched my hand.

She began to speak,

but I couldn't seem to understand.

She said that my sister was

experimenting with a new drug.

She showed me the proof,

it was lying on the rug.

She said that she took much more

than her body could take,

but I knew this wasn't true

it had to be a mistake.

I knew they were wrong,

I wanted to scream.

This all seemed like a bad,

scary, crazy dream.

But I looked at my sister

and I knew it was real.

I didn't know what to do,

I didn't know how to feel.

My only sister lay dead

on her bedroom floor,

and I knew I would not

talk to her anymore.

I looked at my sister

and I began to cry,

and I couldn't stop asking

myself "why?".

Why would she do something

she knew was so wrong.

She knew drugs were bad

for her,

she knew it all along.

But yet and still she was no

longer alive.

All because of a drug

she just had to try.

I didn't know how she

could've been so naïve.

The things my parents said

she must not have believed.

I gathered up my strength

and walked to where my sister lay.

There were some things I

wanted to say.

I told her I loved her,

and told her she would be missed.

And then I said goodbye

and gave her a farewell kiss.

I watched as they carried

my sister out of the room,

delivering her to her eternal doom.

And I couldn't stop crying

because I had just said goodbye,

to my older sister

who was too young to die.

And I began to scream

to let out all the pain,

because I knew I would

never see her again.

Now, it has been one year

since my sister passed away.

And I will never forget

that horrible day.

And I won't let others

forget as well,

because my sister left me with

a story to tell.

<u>Not Alone</u>

The universe wraps

her arms around me

giving me all the love I need.

At night I talk

to her son the moon,

and he listens

intently as I pour out

my heart.

In the day I talk

to her daughter the sun,

and she shines her

beautiful light

on me,

making me feel

all warm and loved.

The universe and

her family are my protectors.

They love me,

and care for me.

They keep me company.

They are my true friends,

my real friends.

They are the reason

I am not alone.

I Said No

Violated and manipulated,

taken for granted,

I was abused.

I said no,

he continued to touch me.

I said no,

he continued to kiss me.

I said no,

I felt his hands forcefully grip my arms.

I screamed no,

he continued anyway.

I feel so dirty.

I wash,

but the feeling doesn't go away.

I cry,

but I still feel the pain.

I want to scream

and let out all the hurt.

I feel so withdrawn and confused.

I want to tell, but I'm so afraid.

If I tell my parents,

what will they say?

If I tell my friends,

what will they think?

He told me if I tell that

he would deny it,

and say that I agreed to it.

I feel a wave of mixed emotions.

If I don't tell,

he'll be free to do this

to someone else.

And if I do tell,

will anyone believe me?

I feel so worthless.

It feels like a precious

part of me was

violently taking away.

It's all my fault

I shouldn't have agreed

to go out with him.

I should've stayed home.

Why me?

Why did something like

this happen to me?

I'm so afraid to trust anyone.

What's going to happen

to me?

I might get pregnant, or worse,

maybe a STD.

My whole life will be

shattered because of this.

I have to tell,

I can't keep this to myself.

It's too much to hold on to.

I can't let him do this

to someone else.

He took something precious

that belonged to me.

And I will not let him do it

to someone else.

I have a responsibility to tell

so he won't do this again.

This shouldn't have happened

because I told him no.

But he wouldn't listen,

he kept on doing what he felt.

And that is not my fault

because

I said NO!!!!!!

ABC Philosophy of Life

Adore…

Beautify….

Cherish…..

Delight in….

Embrace…..

Fulfill…..

Gratify….

Honor…..

Indulge in…..

Journey through….

Kindle…..

Live……

Motivate….

Nurture……

Occupy……

Pursue…….

Qualify…..

Respect…..

Savor......

Treasure....

Utilize.......

Visualize....

Welcome.....

X-perience.....

Yearn for.....

Zest up.....

Your Life

Emotional Whirl

I am lost in a

world of emotions.

Feelings fly,

moments pass,

and thoughts roll by.

I am trapped in an emotional whirl.

At times I want to cry.

At others I want to laugh.

Sometimes I want to scream,

but I don't know how.

I feel a wave of mixed

emotions

and I can't express them all.

I just wonder why they won't flow.

Maybe it's the emotional whirl.

<u>Words of Wisdom</u>

Each day we make

choices,

whether they are

right or wrong.

Each day is full of decisions

we must make,

and choices that will

affect our lives.

Making the right choice

is not always easy,

which is why sometimes

we make mistakes.

But the mistakes we

make are a lesson to us;

to show us the consequences

of our actions.

These mistakes are made

for us to learn from,

for us to be wiser

and smarter,

the next time around.

True Hero

Bravery before fear.

Courage before sorrow.

Fighting to save unknown lives,

knowing for you there would be no tomorrow.

With strength and honor,

you put your lives in danger.

Although you were victims,

you also became saviors.

Mothers, fathers, husbands, wives

daughters, and sons;

you did the unthinkable

and became the miraculous ones.

You had mixed emotions,

many tears you cried.

But you made a choice

and acted it out with pride.

Today America wants to say thank you,

for you all played an important part.

You will always be remembered,

forever heroes in our hearts.

*Dedicated to the passengers & crew of flight 93 and to the FDNY and NYPD**

Perception

Everything

I am

is what I'm not.

The distorted

perception

of my existence

and purpose.

Seeing

beyond what

is seen,

knowing the things

untold.

Everything

I'm not

is what I am.

Causing me to

believe that

things

aren't as they seem.

Dig

Deeper...

Harder.....

Longer....

Stronger....

To find,

to visualize

The truth

that's a lie.

The misconception

of me

draws me to

a well that's

so shallow,

but yet deep.

But can you see?

Everything I am

is what I'm not

Closer,

is where

you see me

coming to

terms with reality.

Because things aren't

always as they seem.

Deception is the key.

Everything

I am is what

I'm not.

Everything I'm not

is what I am.

But can I see????

Reflection

When you look at me

what do you see?

Do you see another person?

Or do you see deep down within me?

Can you see all of my fears,

my hopes and dreams?

Or can you see a person

who is just like you?

Do you see a number in this world

that many people will never know?

I'll tell you what I see

when I look at me.

I see

a dreamer, a giver

a heart, a believer

a helping hand in this world.

This is who I am, and I am me.

To Decide Suicide

A world of darkness,

a world of despair.

There's no hope for me

and no one seems to care.

I walk around

not knowing which way to go.

I'm in a constant daze

but no one seems to know.

My insides are twisted,

my world is bad as can be.

But outward I am fine

there's nothing wrong with me.

For days I walk around

in this state of mind.

Feeling like there's no way out,

no escape to find.

I have tried to fix this problem

over and over again.

But all it leads to is

more pain, anger and frustration.

So now I must come up with a solution

that I think will be the best.

One that will give me ease

and let me be at rest.

I know what that is,

I know what has to be done.

The decision that has to be made

is not an easy one.

I must end it all,

I have to end my life.

That is the only way

I can get rid of this pain and strife.

So I reach for the knife

that is already in my hand.

And my wrist I began to slice

the pain I can stand.

As the pain gets stronger

And my blood begins to fall.

I realize that this

is not what I want at all.

Now I am very dizzy,

and I began to cry.

Because now I really know

I don't want to die!!!!

The Self-Conception of Me

The image of

me

causes such misery.

The conception

of self

I cannot accept.

The impressionable

mind

turns me against myself.

My self-worth,

Is there none?

Images torment me.

My lack thereof

forever haunts me.

The once believable

is forever gone.

Know I not

who I am?

Wanting the me

I can't have,

the me I can't be.

The view of life

I cannot see.

Pretending to be…………..

Forever wanting to be………….

Someone else who's not me………

Is it that

I'm my

own worst enemy?

Dreams

There is a dream

to achieve,

a wandering

soul to find.

Searching to locate

the being itself,

along the rigorous road

that creates

a smooth cruel

pathway ahead.

The process by which

one learns

is not the process

that is learned.

The exaggeration

of life

is the beginning of truth.

To muster up

the courage

to find the unbelievable.

To be in that familiar

room

where change lingers

in the air.

The entrapment of

the past

is the release

of the future.

A dream is the

hope for tomorrow.

High

Silent,

about the

deepest darkest

thoughts.

Scared

to acknowledge

the dilemma that causes

the problems that befalls

this society.

I take one step

forward towards

the future-

Fall down,

and run back to

the past.

Climbing the mountain

is hard.

Falling is not the issue.

Not addressing

the possibility

of failure is the

set back.

Trying to reach

the peak

is my goal.

The goal I eat,

sleep,

dream,

and think about.

It's so close

I can taste it.

So near,

I can smell it.

Right there,

where I can hear.

But being blind

is causing

me to forget

to pick up

solutions

along the way.

Problems

are waiting up ahead,

but can I deal?

Can I reach

the top

if there is a failure

to acknowledge

the silence?

What is success,

if there's no one

to share with,

no one to be

happy?

My inability to see

the disability

that causes

such a fatality

among my

nationality

causes me to slowly

slip and fall.

Am I really

so hIgh iɴ the sky?

Essence of Life

Sometimes it's hard to deal

with the things life throws our way.

But we must press on

in order to make it through each day.

Sometimes we may be dealt

some really tough blows.

But we have to keep going on

through the highs and the lows.

Our life is in the present time,

but it holds the future of our souls.

We must learn to preserve it

as well as achieve our greatest goals.

This thing called life isn't always easy to live.

That's why we must struggle to live life,

and life we must struggle to live.

Someone once said when life gives you lemons

take those lemons and make lemonade.

In life if you make the best of each situation

you will accomplish a lot and achieve the highest grade

So if this book has taught

you anything of essence,

take what you learned

and let your life be your lesson.

Acknowledgements

I would like to take the time to thank everyone who helped me with this project. First, I would like to thank God because without Him I would have no talent or words to express. To my dad, Bobby Whitaker, thank you for encouraging me to do my best. To Ashley, Brittany, Timothy, and Joey, thank you for being my critics and always encouraging me. You four are great siblings (well sometimes anyway☺). To my grandmother Pastor Carolyn Frasier, thank you for your love, support and prayers. To my aunty Wanda Dozier, I want to thank you for all your support and for always being there when I need you. I would like to thank my Uncle Steve "Life" Williams of Lifeline Management for believing in me and encouraging me to get this book out. To my BIG family thank you guys for all your encouragement and support. I wish I could name you all but there are way too many... And last but not least, I want to acknowledge the love of my life, my husband Keashún Derico. Thank you for always standing by my side and believing in me even when I didn't believe in myself. Your love and support has motivated me to speak out and let the world hear my voice. This book is my gift to you!

www.ingramcontent.com/pod-product-compliance
Lightning Source LLC
Chambersburg PA
CBHW031856090426
42741CB00005B/519